Genetics

Jenny Vaughan

W
FRANKLIN WATTS
LONDON•SYDNEY

First published in 2008 by Franklin Watts

Copyright © Franklin Watts 2008

Franklin Watts
338 Euston Road
London NW1 3BH

Franklin Watts Australia
Level 17/207 Kent Street
Sydney NSW 2000

A CIP catalogue record for this book
is available from the British Library.

Dewey number: 567.5

ISBN: 978 0 7496 8267 5

Printed in China

Franklin Watts is a division of Hachette Children's Books,
an Hachette Livre UK company.

www.hachettelivre.co.uk

Consultant: Dr Ruth Newbury-Ecob
Design: Billin Design Solutions
Editor in Chief: John C. Miles
Editor: Sarah Ridley
Art Director: Jonathan Hair
Picture research: Diana Morris

Picture credits:
Bernd Arnold/Visum/Still Pictures: 26. Bill Barksdale/Agstockusa/SPL: 1, 25, 48. Biofoto Associates/SPL: 13tr. John
Carnemolla/Australian Picture Library/Corbis: 17. Nick Cobbing /Rex Features: 9b. Malcolm Croft/PA Photos: 30. Eye of Science/SPL:
8. David Fisher/Rex Features: 39t. Darren Fletcher/The Sun/NI Syndication: 36. Monika Graff/Image Works/Topfoto: 37. Klaus
Guldbrandsen/SPL: 19t. James King-Holmes/SPL: 2-3, 20. David Hosking/FLPA Images: 39b. Hulton-Deutsch Collection/Corbis: 22.
IBL/Rex Features: 16bl. IFFCA: 23. ITV Archive/Rex Features: 21b. Nils Jorgensen/Rex Features: 41t. KPA/Zuma/Rex Features: 11.
Martin McCullough/Rex Features: 31t. Matt Meadows & Peter Arnold/SPL: 24. Newsix/Rex Features: 14b. Oak Ridge National
Laboratory/US dept of Energy/SPL: 28. Alfred Pasieka/SPL: front cover c, 19b. Picturepoint/Topfoto: 38. Pixshots/Shuttertock: 13bl.
Philippe Plailly/Eurelios/SPL: 41b. Prisma/Vupics/Topfoto: 12. Rex Features: 14t, 29, 31b, 33, 46-47. Salamanderman/Shuttertock: 27.
Peter Scoones/SPL: 40. Dr Jurgen Scriba/SPL: 9t. Michael Siluk/Image Works/Topfoto: 34. Carl de Souza/Rex Features: 16tr. SPL: 10,
18. Michael Stephens/PA Photos: 32. Tek Image/SPL: fr cover background. Ullstein/Topfoto: 15. USDA /SPL: 21t. World History
Archive/Topfoto: 35.

CONTENTS

SHINING MICE AND SUPER CROPS

HAVE YOU EVER seen a luminous mouse? Or a tomato that won't rot, or a giant mouse that is part human? Or a field of crops that have extraordinary powers to resist pests and diseases?

GENETICS

All these exist – or have existed – but none of them naturally. They were created by scientists who study genetics – the science of genes. Genes are chemical messages that lie deep in the cells of living things, and which make them what they are – humans, mice, tomatoes… whatever else they might be. They are passed from parents to young.

GENETIC MODIFICATION

In nature, one kind of living thing can only produce young of the same kind as itself (that is, humans can only have human babies, not puppies or kittens). However, scientists have found ways of introducing genes from altogether different living things into certain plants and animals. This is called genetic modification (GM) – and it is how those luminous and giant mice came into being.

▲ This mouse has been genetically modified to make it luminous – able to glow in the dark.

GM has potentially many positive uses but, as we see in the news, there are many fears and concerns about this area of science:

- What if strange animals escape, breed, and create a whole new race of creatures?
- What if the GM crops cross-breed with traditional ones?
- What will be the long-term effects? Are GM crops safe?
- Are we "playing God" – and, if we are, is it right?

CRIMES AND CRIMINALS

The study of genetics has made it possible for the tiniest scraps of human tissue to be used to identify long-dead bodies, help catch murderers – or prove someone's innocence. Yet, even here, there are questions. How reliable is it? And how much information about our genes should the police, or the government, have?

IN OUR GENES?

Finally, there is another big question. If our genes make us who we are, how much do they affect our health and our characters? Can we really choose to do right or wrong – or are we at the mercy of our genes?

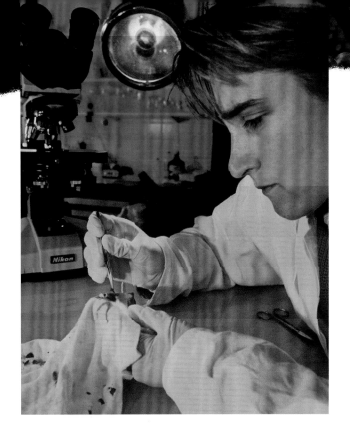

▲ Studying human tissue and identifying its genetic make-up can provide evidence in solving crimes.

▼ Environmental protesters trash GM crops being trialled in a field.

GET THE FACTS STRAIGHT

- All living things contain genes.
- Species of living things that are very alike have similar genes. For example, the genes of humans and chimpanzees are very similar.
- No two living things have exactly the same genes, but identical twins have almost identical genes.

HISTORY 1: BLASPHEMY!

▲ Darwin's belief that humans and apes share a common ancestor is now widely accepted. At the time, however, it was ridiculed – as this contemporary cartoon illustrates.

IN 1859, the English naturalist, Charles Darwin (1809-1882), published a shocking book. Called *On the Origin of Species by Means of Natural Selection*, it challenged the belief, widely held among Christians, that the story of creation in the Bible is literally true. This belief is called "creationism".

FROM MONKEY TO MAN?

Darwin suggested that living things were not created just as they are today by God, but that they change over time, in order to survive. This theory is "evolution by natural selection". Darwin proposed it after visiting the remote Galapagos Islands in the Pacific, where he found species of animals that existed nowhere else. For example, each island had its own kind of finch, with a different sort of beak – just right for the kind of food available. Darwin suggested that plants and animals sometimes develop an extra "something" that helps them survive. They pass this on to their offspring and, over time, a new species evolves.

Darwin and his supporters went on to challenge the Christian belief that humans were created exactly as they are

GET THE FACTS STRAIGHT

- Darwin was not the only scientist to realise that living things evolve. His grandfather, Erasmus Darwin (1731-1802), and the French scientist, Jean-Baptiste Lamarck (1744-1829), were just two scientists who realised this happened, but did not understand how.

- Darwin only published his theory when he found that another naturalist, Alfred Russel Wallace (1823-1913), had come to the same conclusion – but with less evidence. Wallace became one of Darwin's strongest supporters.

now, "in the image of God". Instead, we, too, have evolved – and share a common ancestor with apes and monkeys. It was blasphemy! Darwin was bitterly attacked and ridiculed – but, today, no serious scientists doubt him.

FUNDAMENTALISTS

Some religious fundamentalists still reject the theory of evolution. These include Mike Huckabee, who campaigned in 2007/8 to become a candidate to be US president. A CBS poll in 2004 showed 37% of Americans wanted creationism (or a version of it called "intelligent design", which does not mention God) to be taught in schools as an alternative to evolution. Fifty-five per cent said they believed God created humans as we are today.

In the last 10 years, at least 20 US states have objected to the teaching of evolution as fact, and there have been high-profile disputes. In 2007, when the education authorities in Kansas voted narrowly to remove alternative ideas to evolution from their science guidelines, 4,000 people petitioned in protest.

▼ Mike Huckabee campaigning in 2007 to become a US presidential candidate. Huckabee rejects Darwin's theory of evolution.

HISTORY 2: PARENTS AND OFFSPRING

DARWIN KNEW that living things inherit characteristics from their parents. In 1866, an Austrian monk named Gregor Mendel (1822-1884) published his important discoveries.

YELLOW PEAS, GREEN PEAS

Mendel studied pea plants – some with yellow peas and some with green. Seeds form when the female part of a flower is fertilised with pollen from the male part. Mendel discovered that, if the yellow-pea flowers were fertilised with pollen from green-pea flowers, all the peas that formed were yellow. He grew new plants from these, and fertilised them with their own pollen, expecting that the peas resulting would be like their "parent". He was surprised to find that some produced green peas. It was as if the greenness had been hiding in the plant. Mendel realised that living things can inherit "hidden" traits from their parents.

▲ Gregor Mendel made important discoveries about inheritance – yet, after his death, his work remained forgotten for nearly 50 years.

AFTER MENDEL

Scientists later found that the cells of living things contain tiny rod-shaped bodies called chromosomes. We now know that humans have 23 pairs of chromosomes which, as with all living things, are in the centre, or nucleus, of almost every cell in the body.

Chromosomes contain packages of information that cause living things to inherit characteristics from their parents. These are our "genes", which are set out on the chromosomes like beads on a necklace. Mendel's work had showed that some genes

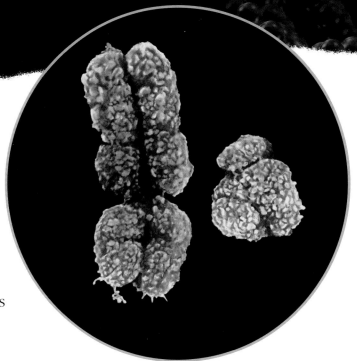

some genes are "dominant" – which means their effects are likely to show up if one parent carries them. Others are "recessive", which means they can hide, like the greenness of some pea plants. To show up, they must be inherited from both parents. Knowing this has helped scientists work out how to breed new strains of plants and animals, and how certain diseases pass on through generations.

X AND Y CHROMOSOMES

One pair of chromosomes is responsible for making us male or female. They are the X and Y sex chromosomes. Males have one X and one Y; in females, both are X.

▲ The X-chromosome is shown on the left, the Y is the smaller one, on the right.

GET THE FACTS STRAIGHT

Mendel discovered that when he crossed a yellow pea with a green one, all the offspring were yellow. Yellow was the dominant gene. However:

- Each one of this first generation of pea plants had one recessive "hidden" green gene.

- He then "self fertilised" these plants (so no genes from other plants were involved). In each case, one of every four offspring was all green, one was all yellow with no green gene, and the rest were yellow with the hidden green gene. The proportions were always the same when there was a recessive green gene.

▲ Dominant genes ensure these puppies look like their mother.

USING INHERITANCE – FOR BETTER AND WORSE

SINCE ANCIENT TIMES, even before people knew the theory of genetics, they understood how it worked in practice.

EARLY FARMERS

Early farmers developed wheat, maize, barley and other grain crops from wild grasses, through careful breeding. They bred domestic farm animals from their wild counterparts – boar, wild cattle and sheep – and horses ranging from tiny Shetland ponies to huge cart-horses. People attempted a similar idea among themselves. Aristocrats and rich people encouraged their children only to marry people like themselves. This was partly to keep wealth in the family – but partly because they really believed they were superior, and had "breeding".

▲ A coat of arms may include the symbols of the different ancestors of an aristocratic family.

▼ In 2008, Australian Prime Minister Kevin Rudd apologised to the Aboriginal people for the country's past policy of stealing their children to "civilise" them.

"SUPERMEN" AND WOMEN

The idea took a sinister turn in the late-19th and early-20th centuries with the rise of "eugenics". This suggested that only the "best" people should have children, and that whole sections of the human race should be discouraged from doing so. Laws that allowed people considered "feeble-minded" to be sterilised – made unable to have children – were passed in the first half of the 20th century in many countries, including the USA, France and Sweden.

In Australia between 1910 and the 1970s, thousands of Aboriginal children of mixed race, usually where the mother was Aboriginal and the father white, were cruelly taken from their parents and placed in white families or orphanages. This was an attempt to "breed out" their blackness, and to "civilise" them.

▲ The Nazis applied the ideas of eugenics when they decided to imprison and murder millions of Jews and others considered "unacceptable" in concentration camps.

FACING THE ISSUES

In the 19th century, even serious scientists believed that some human "races" are more developed than others. Modern geneticists disagree. Professor Steve Jones of University College, London says that, while there are many inherited differences between humans, most differences can be found within all so-called races. "Race," he says, "is a fairly meaningless concept."
(*The Language of Genes*, 1993)

Eugenics was at its worst in the 1930s in Germany when the Nazis murdered millions of Jews, gypsies, disabled people and others they considered unacceptable. At the same time, chosen men and women were encouraged to breed a blond, blue-eyed "master-race".

The idea of breeding better humans has not completely died out. In 2007, *The Times* reported that some British men have paid over £30,000 to American university students to become surrogate mothers for them, hoping that this will guarantee intelligent babies. (It does not.)

ANIMAL ODDITIES, PECULIAR PLANTS

BREEDING ANIMALS and plants to suit humans have brought about some strange results, such as giant vegetables, turkeys too heavy to fly and cows that produce 10 times more milk than they need for their calves.

▼ Humans have bred an extraordinary variety of different dogs. This tiny chihuahua is only a fraction of the size of the huge wolf-hound – but they are both descended from wolves.

▲ Huge vegetables like this giant leek are the result of careful breeding and special treatment as they grow.

A DOG'S LIFE

All dogs are descended from wolves. Yet, over the centuries, people have bred a range of creatures that look almost nothing like their wild ancestors: Pekingese like tiny lions, pugs that can hardly breathe, chihuahuas smaller than cats and giant Great Danes with hearts too weak to carry them into old age. Many breeds of dogs were developed for certain jobs: terriers were bred to catch rats, and greyhounds to run fast.

Often, breeding aims to produce valuable pedigree dogs, using a small selection of animals that have characteristics that will win them prizes at shows, and so make money for the breeders. This is called using a small gene pool. The characteristics the dogs are valued for become exaggerated and the animals may suffer from inherited problems. In 2004, one vet told a television programme: "Modern bulldogs can't run... they can't give birth. They have enormous problems with too much soft tissue in their mouth and it adds up to a dog that is struggling for air all its life."

▲ The wrinkly skins of these Merino sheep mean they can produce more wool – but are more likely to suffer from painful fly strike.

WRINKLY SHEEP

Farm animals have not fared much better. For example, Merino sheep have been bred to have very wrinkly skin – because more skin can produce more wool. But sweat and urine become trapped in the wrinkles, attracting flies, whose maggots burrow into the sheep's flesh. This is called fly strike. Some farmers in Australia try to prevent this by cutting away part of the sheeps' flesh, without using any anaesthetic. In 2005, animal rights groups organised boycotts of Australian wool in protest. Farmers are now looking for other ways to prevent fly strike.

WHAT DO YOU THINK?

People have bred farm animals and pets to suit human needs or wants for thousands of years.

⬛ Do you think it is right to breed animals that may have some health problems - but which can help provide food, or do work for humans, or make good pets?

⬛ Imagine you are planning a pet show. What would you look for in the pets? Good "breeding" or something else?

DURING the first part of the 20th century, a number of scientists studying genes realised that they are made up of molecules (tiny particles) of a chemical called deoxyribonucleic acid (DNA).

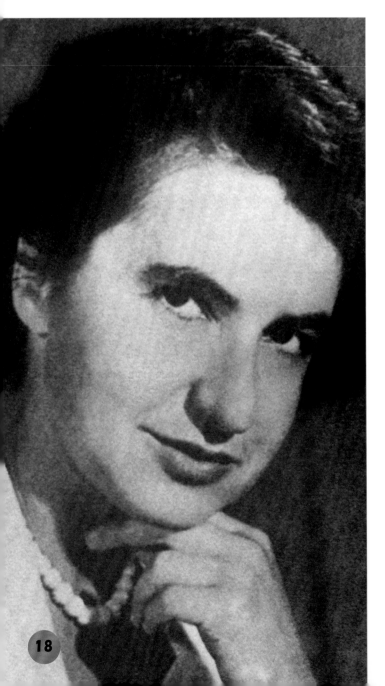

ONE "DARK LADY" AND THREE MEN

Our genes are groups of these molecules, which are inside our chromosomes (see page 13). A big breakthrough in the study of DNA came in the early 1950s, when a young scientist at London University, named Rosalind Franklin (1920-1958), managed to take a photograph of an X-ray of the DNA molecule. This showed that it is a double helix: this looks a bit like a twisted ladder – a pair of long strands with "rungs" connecting them. Franklin's colleague, Maurice Wilkins, showed the photograph to Cambridge scientists, Francis Crick (1916-2004) and James Watson (1928-).

◄ Rosalind Franklin's X-ray photograph of a DNA molecule was vital to understanding DNA, and many people think that her work in this field was so important that she should be considered one of the discoverers of DNA. However, she felt that, as a woman, she was sidelined by the scientific establishment, and moved away into other areas of study, until her early death.

THE KEY TO INHERITANCE

Using Franklin's X-ray image, Crick and Watson discovered that the "rungs" in the DNA are the key to inheritance. They are made up of pairs of chemicals, called bases. These are the chemicals adenine (A), guanine (G), cytosine (C) and thymine (T). A is always linked with T, and C with G. The order in which these pairs appear in DNA works like a code that tells the cells in a living thing how to make the proteins which make it grow, break down food, absorb oxygen from the air – all the things it needs to do to stay alive. Cells are constantly splitting in two in order to grow, or to replace cells that have died. As each cell splits, it gets half of the double helix, which is copied, to make a new double helix – the same as the original, and carrying the same information.

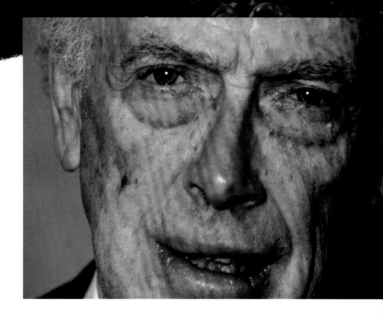

▲ In 2007 James Watson, one of the pioneers of understanding DNA, caused an outcry by suggesting that black people are genetically less intelligent than white people. Ironically, it appears that Watson himself has African ancestors.

▼ This photograph shows clearly the "double helix" form of the DNA molecule.

GET THE FACTS STRAIGHT

- We have about three billion base pairs (6 billion bases total) of DNA in most of our cells.

- The differences between us – even really obvious ones, like the colour of our skin or our height – are caused by only about 3 million base pairs. That is only one-tenth of one per cent of our DNA.

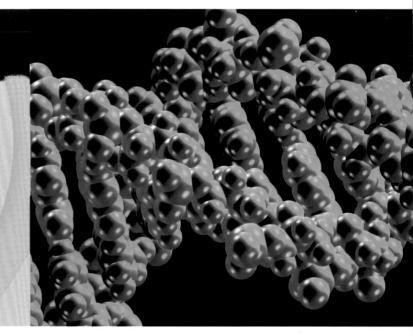

THE CHANGING CODE

THE CODE, or order in which the bases appear, is different in every kind of living thing. That means, for example, the code in a cat's DNA is different from that of a human (though not, as it happens, by very much).

▲ The DNA code can be represented as a pattern of letters. This picture shows part of the code for a human.

DNA CODES

DNA codes also differ between individuals of the same species. So, as humans, our DNA is slightly different from anyone else's – it is unique to us. The closest it is ever likely to be to anyone else's is if we have an identical twin. This is because these twins start life as a single cell, with a single pattern of DNA, which then splits into two. Living things pass their DNA on to their young, who then have similar DNA to their parents, and look rather like them.

However, the code in their DNA can suddenly change a lot, or "mutate", so that there is something noticeably different about the young. This mutation may be harmful – or useful. For example, a bird may be born with a beak a little more suitable for eating the food available – which is how the finches that Darwin noticed came to evolve. This is how all living creatures have evolved over millions of years.

DECAY

DNA also changes with age. This is as true for humans as every other living thing. All through our life our cells are dividing, and the DNA in them is splitting and copying itself. The more often this happens, the more chances there are for mistakes to happen to it. This is why, as we grow older, we are more likely to become weak or ill. Modern medicine can keep more and more of us alive into old age – but this has created a big problem for society. How do we care for larger and larger numbers of fragile old people, who are more likely to be unable to look after themselves?

▼ As we age, more and more mistakes appear in our DNA – resulting in increasing weakness and ill-health.

▲ Mutations have made some of these fruit flies vary slightly from each other.

WHAT DO YOU THINK?

As we age, our DNA develops the mistakes that eventually kill us. If we could stop this happening, we could, in theory live much, much longer.

◘ Do you think this is a good idea?

◘ Why might it be a bad idea?

◘ How might we change the way we live if we could count on having much longer lives?

UNLUCKY INHERITANCE

◀ Tsar Nicholas of Russia, his wife Alexandra and their children – all of whom were murdered in 1918, during the Russian Revolution. Their son, Alexei, had the genetic condition haemophilia. It was passed to him by his mother – who was herself unaffected.

MANY DISEASES are caused by "mistakes" in recessive genes. Understanding them is key to helping carriers and sufferers of these inherited conditions.

RECESSIVE GENES

Cystic fibrosis is caused by a recessive gene (see page 13), and affects about one child in 2,500 in Europe. This inherited condition causes the lungs to fill with mucus and easily become infected. The digestive system often does not work properly, and the person may die young.

Sickle cell disease, a painful blood condition, is also caused by a recessive gene. If both parents carry this recessive gene, each of their children has a one-in-four chance that they will be affected. If the parents are closely related, this increases the chance of them both carrying the gene.

WHAT DO YOU THINK?

It is now becoming clear that many dangerous diseases or conditions - such as heart disease and some cancers - have their roots in our DNA. We might want to know if we are at risk of such conditions - if we can use that knowledge to protect ourselves. But what if a test shows you are carrying the gene for a fatal condition and there is nothing you can do about it? Would you want to know?

X CHROMOSOMES AND DISEASE

Many inherited diseases result from mutations in genes on the X sex chromosome. A woman has two of these. If one carries a mistake, the other one – which doesn't – can mask its effects, and the woman is healthy. As males have no second X chromosome, such diseases are more common in boys. An example is haemophilia, when sufferers' blood fails to clot properly. Without treatment, the slightest injury puts them in danger of bleeding to death. In the 1800s, this gene appeared in Queen Victoria's family, and eventually passed on to Alexei, the son of the last Tsar of Russia.

TESTING IN PREGNANCY

Doctors can offer tests for many genetic conditions and parents may choose to end a pregnancy, should they discover their unborn child is carrying an inherited condition. Doctors may also test for the condition Down's syndrome. This occurs when a child has 47 chromosomes instead of 46, because they have an extra copy of chromosome 21. This results in various possible health problems and learning difficulties. Many people oppose ending such pregnancies, saying it is judging that a disabled life is not worth as much as an able-bodied one.

► Dr Tom Shakespeare's very short stature is caused by a genetic condition called achondroplasia. As a disability campaigner, he has expressed concern that mothers can be pressured into ending pregnancies if the baby seems likely to be disabled.

FRANKENSTEIN FOODS?

LIKE OTHER living things, plants usually inherit genes from other plants like themselves. But science has changed this – and, in many parts of the world, genetically modified (GM) crops are being grown. Many people are very suspicious of these. They call foods made from them "Frankenstein foods" after a science fiction story of a mad scientist who created a monster.

HOW IT IS DONE

One way to genetically modify a plant is by infecting it with a kind of bacteria, which makes its way into the plant's genes. Normally, the bacteria produce tumours in the plant but scientists have removed the tumour-causing genes from the bacteria and replaced them with useful ones. The plants are then infected with the bacteria, which carry the new, useful genes into their cells. Another way is to fire tiny gold particles coated with useful genes into the cells of the plants, using something called a "gene gun". When new plants are bred from genetically modified plants they all contain the new, useful genes.

◄ A scientist "infects" plant cells with new DNA, using a gene gun.

WHY IS IT DONE?

Some GM crops are made to produce higher yields. Some are resistant to herbicides (weed-killer), so farmers can spray the fields without killing the crops. This makes more space and more water for the crops – which also helps increase yields. Supporters of GM crops say they need less herbicide than traditional crops – so they are actually good for the environment. Some plants have been modified to produce a poison that kills pests that feed on them. This means the crop can

▲ Genetically-modified crops can sprayed with herbicide (weed-killer) and not be damaged by it.

be grown without using pesticides – which may also be better for the environment, and for anyone who has to work with the crops. Scientists are also able to modify some plants so that they will manufacture medicines in their cells – which can be extracted and given to people as pills.

GET THE FACTS STRAIGHT

- Genetically modified crops are widely grown in the United States, Canada and South America. The most commonly grown GM foods are soya and maize, and around 70% of foods in the US contain GM products.

- By contrast, many countries within Europe, including Britain, only allow GM crops to be grown on a trial, rather than a commercial, basis.

DANGEROUS MEDDLING?

SUPPORTERS of GM crops believe that they will provide the world with much-needed food. When accused of meddling with nature, they say that crops have been cross-bred for many thousands of years, and are already unlike anything found in the wild. What is the problem?

▼ Crops damaged by drought. Supporters of GM crops say new breeds can withstand drought better.

ARE THEY SAFE?

Opponents point out that GM crops are far more "unnatural" than traditional crops. They contain genes that could never have found their way into a plant through pollen – they may even be animal genes. No one knows what the long-term effects may be. GM crops might be damaging to our health and the health of wildlife by spreading into the environment.

In 2004, the European Union lifted a ban on GM foods – but there is protest wherever they are grown. In 2008, President Sarkozy of France announced that the only GM crops grown commercially in France, a type of maize, would be banned. In 2002, safety fears led the government of Zambia to ban US donations of corn, even though the country faced famine.

FACING THE ISSUES

In 2005, modified genes from GM rape (a plant related to cabbages) found its way into a weed called the charlock – which was almost impossible to kill. This event provided opponents of GM crops with evidence to support their views.

FARMERS' INCOMES

Opponents also argue that GM will not really help provide food for the world, and will harm farmers' incomes. This is because GM seeds are expensive, but farmers may find that, to be competitive, they must use them – and so their profits will fall. Also, if GM crops are planted in open fields, their pollen can spread to traditional crops. Many people prefer to buy these traditional crops and will pay higher prices for food grown in this way, but not if the crops are pollinated by GM crops. Thirdly, there is the danger that GM crops could interbreed with weeds, developing "super-weeds", resistant to pests and diseases. Farmers would then need to use more pesticide and herbicide rather than less. There are fewer worries over crops that have been bred to contain medicines, as these are usually grown in closed greenhouses, and are not for direct sale.

▶ Some GM crops – usually ones that are being bred to create medicine – are grown in closed greenhouses. These pose less of a threat to the environment than those grown in an open field.

27

MAKING MONSTERS?

GENETICALLY modified animals have, so far, been produced mainly for medical and scientific research rather than for food. But this is likely to change in the near future, and we will have to decide whether or not we find breeding GM farm animals acceptable. The creation of such animals is likely to create even more controversy than the development of GM crops.

► The giant mouse (left) has been genetically modified with rat genes, which make it grow bigger.

HOW IS IT DONE?

Animals can be genetically modified by injecting DNA from one species into the fertilised egg of another. This egg is then implanted into the womb of a "surrogate mother". The developing young animal carries the genes from another living thing, which it passes on to future generations. We say such animals are "transgenic". There have been transgenic pigs, sheep, poultry, fish, insects and even monkeys. The largest number of transgenic animals so far have been mice.

WHY IS IT DONE?

Mice that contain human DNA can be used to test a range of drugs, including some for cancer. Animals have also been genetically modified, like some plants, to make medicines. For example, sheep have been bred to produce milk that can help treat cystic fibrosis, and milk from rabbits with some DNA can be used to treat children with Pompe's disease, a fatal muscular condition. Pigs with human DNA may in the future be able to provide body organs, such as hearts, for transplant. This is called xenotransplantation.

WEIRD AND NOT-SO-WONDERFUL

GM animals include pigs with green trotters, teeth and eyes, and which glow – and rabbits and kittens that do the same. These have been produced using DNA from jellyfish. The idea is that genetic material from the glowing jellyfish can be put into other animals, along with other, useful genes. The "luminous" genes act as a marker, to show up the useful genes, which can then easily be seen as they develop.

▲ The piglet on the left contains jellyfish genes, so that it will glow green in the dark.

But genetic manipulation in animals, however useful, is tricky, prone to mistakes and can produce unwanted effects. Some GM pigs, for example, suffer from joint disease and heart problems, or have grown so big their legs cannot support them. As with crops, there is also a danger of GM animals escaping and breeding with "normal" animals – making a change in nature that can never be reversed.

WHAT DO YOU THINK?

Genetically modified animals developed for medical reasons can save human lives. But do we have the right to create "unnatural" animals?

● Do you think the fact that these animals will be used to help people makes a difference?

● Is there any real difference between creating special animals – such as pigs to use in transplants – and rearing farm animals for meat?

"FINGERPRINTS"

IN 1984, Professor Sir Alec Jeffreys from the University of Leicester, discovered how to detect the variations between the DNA of individual people. Our DNA is unique to us, just as our fingerprints are unique, so identifying it is called "genetic fingerprinting".

▲ Stefan Kiszko was unjustly imprisoned for a murder committed in 1973. In 1992, DNA evidence was able to prove him innocent. Sadly, he died soon after he was released from prison.

PROOF POSITIVE

Genetic fingerprinting has become important to the police. They examine the scene of the crime for the tiniest scraps of DNA which may lead them to a suspect. DNA fingerprinting is also used to solve crimes that took place in the past. In 1975, 11-year-old Lesley Molseed was found murdered. A man named Stefan Kiszko was jailed for killing her – but, in 1992, he was cleared when DNA evidence proved he could not have committed the crime. In November 2007, DNA evidence was used to convict another man, Ronald Castree.

NOT ALWAYS PERFECT

Although DNA is useful, it has limits. Where there is very little DNA available, a technique called DNA Low Copy Number (DNA LCN) may be used. In 1998, a bomb in the Northern Irish town of Omagh killed 29 people. In December 2007, Sean Hoey was tried for planting it. But the amounts of DNA used as evidence against him were so small that experts said they proved nothing. Hoey was found not guilty. However, DNA LCN is still used in some court cases.

▲ The aftermath of the IRA bomb in Omagh, Northern Ireland. The DNA evidence from the crime was not good enough to convict the main suspect.

TRACING IN SECRET

In the United States, the fact that DNA samples can be collected without a suspect's knowledge has been challenged in court as an invasion of privacy. Saliva left on a cigarette butt or a glass can provide vital evidence – but critics argue that allowing the police to collect such material in secret, unless they can demonstrate that they have very sound reasons to do so, means that innocent people's DNA could become part of police records.

▼ Police search a crime scene for evidence, including any containing DNA.

GET THE FACTS STRAIGHT

- Police in the US have DNA samples from about one per cent of the population – compared with only about 0.3 per cent in most European countries. In Britain, by contrast, the figure is five per cent – including many people arrested but never found guilty of any crime.

- Campaigners in both the US and Britain want to end the right of the police to hold DNA records of innocent people. In Britain, this is being challenged in the European Court.

IT IS POSSIBLE to use the tiny differences between each human being to find out who our relatives are, and gain information about our ancestors.

IMMIGRATION DISPUTES

When Professor Jeffreys discovered genetic fingerprinting, a lawyer in London contacted him, and asked if he could help a woman from Ghana, living with her family in Britain. After one son visited Ghana, he was refused re-entry to Britain. The British authorities said they thought he was not really the woman's son. Professor Jeffreys and his team proved the young man was telling the truth, and he was allowed to re-join his mother. DNA evidence is now often used in immigration disputes. It has also been used in kidnap cases. This happened in 2004 when a Kenyan couple were accused of stealing children and convincing childless couples that they had given birth to "miracle babies". DNA tests proved the babies were not related to their "parents" and helped reunite many of them with their real families.

▶ The Kenyan pastor Dr Gilbert Deya was accused of persuading childless couples that they had given birth to "miracle" children. DNA tests proved that the babies had been stolen.

ROOTS

Finding out about ancestors has been especially important for black people from the Caribbean and North and South America. Between the 16th and 19th centuries, their ancestors were kidnapped in Africa and sold into slavery. Families were split up, people were given "new" names that were not their own and were bought and sold like animals. Many lost touch with their family history.

In fact, everyone can learn about their ancestors from their DNA. The United States, especially, is famous for being a "melting pot" of immigrants, and has a huge number of laboratories to help people discover where their ancestors came from – often specialising in particular groups, such as Jewish people, Italians, or native Americans.

▼ Norwich market, Norfolk. Many families have lived in the region for generations and the local University of East Anglia is taking part in DNA-based research to find out where their ancestors came from.

WHAT DO YOU THINK?

As well as solving crimes, DNA samples can unite people with long-lost relatives and help people learn about their family history.

- Who might want DNA data?
- Why might anyone want to keep their DNA data private?
- How could DNA data be mis-used?

NATURE AND NURTURE

◀ A child takes an "intelligence test". These were once thought to reveal how naturally intelligent people are. But we now know that cultural differences and practice affect performance.

HOW MUCH do we inherit our characters and personalities from our parents – and how much are they the result of our upbringing?

IT'S IN OUR GENES

The idea that people are born with certain character traits is very old. After all, it seems to make sense. We know that some types of dogs are especially fierce. When we read about pit bull terriers attacking children, we remember that these dogs have been bred for fighting. (They have, in fact, also been trained for this.) If animal breeders take it for granted that temperament varies with

breed, why should humans be different? It seems that they are not: children take after their parents in many ways. They may be musical, or artistic, or especially good at maths and science. Troublingly, a tendency to become addicted to cigarettes, drugs or alcohol also seems to run in families. So does obesity. How much can we be held responsible for the way we live our lives?

IT'S OUR UPBRINGING

During much of the 20th century, psychologists moved away from thinking we inherit our characters, to emphasising the importance of upbringing. The only way to test this seemed to be to find identical twins (with almost the same DNA) who were brought up separately. This happens rarely, and it was expected that such twins would be very different from each other. In fact, they seem usually to have very similar personalities. But how much this is down to their genes, and how much is a result of being adopted by similar families is hard to tell.

NO – IT'S BOTH

Most doctors and geneticists now believe that our characters are the result of both our nature (our genes), and our nurture (how we are brought up). As for intelligence and talent – yes, we do inherit these, but diet, illness and life experience also have an effect. The whole question is extremely complicated.

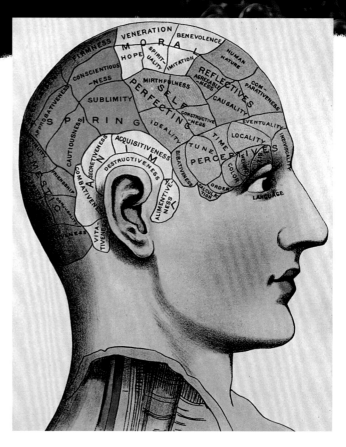

▲ Phrenology was a popular science in the 19th century. People believed that characters were something that humans were born with – as we might say today, the result of the genes. They thought it was possible to learn about people's characters from feeling the shape of the skull.

WHAT DO YOU THINK?

- If our behaviour is affected by our genes, does this mean that people who seem to inherit problem personalities just cannot help themselves?

- What could this mean for how society treats criminals and other people who behave in problematic ways?

ALTERED INHERITANCE

SCIENTISTS NOW REALISE that our genes, our health and our environment act together to affect the way our bodies develop.

◀ Although identical twins Olivia (right) and Isabella Murphy have almost the same DNA as each other, a gene that leads to someone getting leukaemia was active only in Olivia.

SWITCHES

It seems that our environment can "switch on" mutated genes that affect our health. This was shown in January 2008, when scientists announced a breakthrough in understanding a kind of leukaemia (cancer of the blood) that affects children. Isabella and Olivia Murphy are identical twins – with almost exactly the same DNA. But only Olivia developed childhood leukaemia.

Studies showed that both girls had a few cells in their bodies containing a mutated gene that was likely to cause leukaemia. In Olivia, this had become activated – switched on – by another mutation, possibly after a minor infection. Scientists identified the cells with the mutated genes in them. Now they can monitor Isabella for leukaemia, and also target the mutated cells in other children.

EPIGENETICS

Recently, some scientists have begun to suggest that a mother's life experiences can affect the DNA of her baby. Doctors found that babies born to mothers affected by the attacks on New York in 2001 had high levels of stress hormones (chemicals the body produces when it is stressed) in their bodies. They believe that this occurred because something had switched on the gene that told their developing baby's body to produce stress hormones too.

Research suggests that this can last over several generations. Survivors of the concentration camps of the Second World War also had high levels of stress hormones – and so did their children, and even their children's children. It was as if the switch that activated the gene that told the cell to produce this hormone was switched on in one generation, and remained switched on for at least two generations afterwards. This way that our genes (and possibly our descendents' genes) can be altered by things that happen to us is called "epigenetics".

▲ The shock of being close to the 2001 attacks on the World Trade Center had an effect on unborn babies.

GET THE FACTS STRAIGHT

It is commonly said that identical twins share exactly the same DNA. However, this is not quite true. Their DNA is almost identical, but outside influences can cause slight variations, both before and after birth. As the story of the Murphy twins on page 36 shows, such influences can make a big difference in life.

CARBON COPIES

IN 1997, scientists at the Roslin Institute, a research centre that is part of the University of Edinburgh, made a momentous announcement. The year before, they had been the first to create a cloned mammal using a cell from another adult mammal. The clone was a sheep they named Dolly – and the story hit the headlines.

► Dolly, the cloned sheep, became quite a celebrity in her short life – though some scientists believe that problems resulting from cloning may possibly have been responsible for her early death.

CLONES AND CLONING

Clones happen in nature, when cuttings are taken from plants, and when animals (such as humans) give birth to more than one young with virtually identical DNA. When Dolly was born, artificially created clones of other animals had already been made using cells from embryos. What made Dolly different was the use of an adult cell.

Dolly was made using the egg of another sheep, with its nucleus removed. DNA from yet another adult sheep was used to replace the "missing" nucleus, and the egg put into the womb of a surrogate mother sheep. The lamb that resulted was a clone of the adult sheep whose DNA had been used.

AFTER DOLLY

The technique used to clone Dolly has been used many times since – including to make transgenic animals, such as a sheep whose milk can be used to treat haemophilia. But cloning is difficult and dangerous. It has a high failure rate and, very often, the clone has severe health problems. Even Dolly died young – she was put down when she was seven because she had lung problems of a kind normally found in much older sheep. (Though it has been suggested that her illness was perhaps because she spent more time indoors than is natural for a sheep.)

 Identical twins share much of the same DNA, and so, in a sense are almost clones of each other. They look almost exactly the same, and are likely to have similar personalities.

NOT LIVING FOR EVER

Cloning humans is illegal almost everywhere, but there are claims that it has happened. Some Americans have paid huge sums to have favourite pets cloned, hoping to re-create loved ones. But this misunderstands cloning. A clone shares the original's DNA, but it is a separate individual, with a separate life – just as identical twins (who are almost clones of each other) are two different people.

GET THE FACTS STRAIGHT

Since the 1960s, almost all the elm trees in Britain have died from Dutch Elm Disease. The trees were all descended from a single clone, and shared most of the same DNA. None was able to develop any resistance to the disease. This problem of disease spreading easily can affect any breed of plant or animal that shares a lot of DNA. So it is important for farmers and gardeners to use a wide range of strains of crops and animals.

THE FUTURE

THE SCIENCE OF GENETICS is constantly
on the move. Discoveries are being made and new ideas
and techniques are being developed all the time.

WORKING WITH GENES

In 2003, the whole human genome (all the genes on all our chromosomes) was successfully "mapped" – that is, scientists knew which genes occur where. Now, in some cases, genes that do not work properly can be replaced. For example, a condition called Lebers Congenital Amaurosis is caused by a faulty gene that affects the light-detecting cells in the eyes. Eventually, sufferers lose their sight altogether.

In 2008, doctors managed to replace the faulty gene in several patients – and save their sight. This type of treatment is called gene therapy – and it also includes attempts to "turn off" genes that do not work properly. This could lead to better treatments for cancer, for example.

▶ DNA from sea slugs can be used to make it hard for mosquitoes to carry and spread the disease malaria (see next page).

▲ Nobel Prize-winning genetics expert Sir John Sulston believes that discoveries about genetics should be shared among scientists and used for good – not profit.

CHANGING NATURE

Altering the genes of other creatures could also benefit human health. Scientists hope to use GM in the fight against malaria, which kills over a million people a year, and makes 500 million severely ill. Malaria is caused by a parasite carried inside a certain type of mosquito, and is passed onto humans when they are bitten. In December 2007, scientists announced that an animal called a sea cucumber contains a substance in its body that makes it hard for parasites to grow in its gut. Scientists have genetically modified a mosquito using sea slug DNA, so less of the parasite develops. If modified mosquitoes breed with unmodified ones, one day the levels of malaria could be drastically reduced.

NEW ANIMALS

High-quality GM animals could be cloned, so that their DNA can be more widely used in breeding, to create new and better sources of food. Genetically modified creatures might be made to produce larger animals, or ones more resistant to disease. But, as we have seen, all this is very controversial, and there are many people who feel that tampering with nature to this extent is full of unknown dangers.

▼ GM farm animals may become more common – but this might have dangers.

WHAT DO YOU THINK?

Understanding genetics could bring us many benefits – from fighting crime to providing much-needed food for the world and curing killer diseases.

- How can we judge when a technology may do more harm than good?

- Who should be responsible for making sure that cutting-edge science is used for good rather than dangerous reasons?

- Is there a danger that other problems – like getting enough clean drinking water for everyone in the world – will be ignored at the expense of new and exciting sciences?

GLOSSARY

bases/ base pairs Chemicals/pairs of chemicals which, together, make up DNA.

cell The extremely small basic unit that makes up every living thing.

chromosome A strand of DNA that carries the genes.

clone A living thing that has almost exactly the same DNA as another.

DNA Deoxyribonucleic acid, the substance of which most genes are made.

dominant A gene that is likely to show up in a living thing's offspring is "dominant".

double helix A shape like a twisted ladder.

epigenetics The way that things can affect our genes, other than by DNA mutation.

eugenics A belief that the human race can be "improved" by controlling who should or should not have children.

evolution The theory that living things change (or "evolve") over generations to suit their environments better.

fertilise To unite with a female cell in a plant or animal to begin the process of new life.

gene A tiny part of a chromosome, made up of DNA, which influences which characteristics a living thing inherits from its parents.

gene therapy The treatment of a genetic disorder by replacing or "switching off" genes.

genetics The study of genes.

genetic modification Artificially changing the genes in a living thing.

genetic fingerprint The unique pattern of an individual's DNA is called its genetic or DNA fingerprint.

geneticist A scientist who studies genetics.

GM crops Crops produced from original plants that have been genetically modified.

luminous Giving off light.

molecule The smallest particle possible into which a substance can be broken up.

mucus A slimy substance produced by the body – for example, in your nose.

mutate To genetically change – in living things, it can mean developing a new characteristic, or losing one.

natural selection The idea that when a living thing develops characteristics that will help it survive, it is more likely to produce young with the same characteristics.

pesticides Chemicals that kill pests such as insects or bacteria.

phrenology A so-called "science" which suggested that a person's character would show up in the shape of their skull.

recessive A gene that can "hide" in a living thing, and may only show up sometimes in its offspring is "recessive".

surrogate mother A woman who bears a child for another woman.

transgenic A living thing whose body contains genes that would not have been found there naturally.

WEBSITES

To understand genetics, and extend what you have found out from this book, you will find it hard to do better than looking at the GlaxoSmithKline website on the subject. In addition to the Web, where there is a huge number of useful sites, there is a particularly useful book on the subject of genetics: *The Language of Genes*, by Steve Jones, Revised edition published in 2000 by Flamingo.

http://www.genetics.gsk.com
A website produced by the pharmaceutical company GlaxoSmithKline, covering a wide range of information about genetics.

http://www.genewatch.org/index-396405
The site of a campaigning group, "Genewatch".

http://www.biology-online.org/2/11_natural_selection.htm
Helps explain Darwin's theory.

http://www.nhm.ac.uk/nature-online/science-of-natural-history/biographies/charles-darwin/charles-darwin.html
A life of Charles Darwin.

http://anthro.palomar.edu/mendel/mendel_1.htm
About Gregor Mendel.

http://www.bbc.co.uk/history/historic_figures/watson_and_crick.shtml
Crick, Watson and the Discovery of DNA.

http://www.ornl.gov/sci/techresources/Human_Genome/elsi/cloning.shtml
A cloning fact sheet.

http://genome.wellcome.ac.uk/doc_wtd020878.html
About genetic fingerprinting.

Every effort has been made by the Publishers to ensure that the websites in this book are suitable for children, that they are of the highest educational value, and that they contain no inappropriate or offensive material. However, because of the nature of the Internet, it is impossible to guarantee that the contents of these sites will not be altered. We strongly advise that Internet access is supervised by a responsible adult.

INDEX

Here are the lists of contents for each title in *Science in the News*: